Perfectly Imperfect Woman of God
Uniquely You

Karen Pless Gaines

Kiara Espinoza

This book is based on biblical standards and reflect the authors view from her own life experiences. If any part of this book offends anyone it was not done intentional. Maybe it's not for you. Pass it on to someone else.

Copyright © 2023 Karen Pless Gaines

The scanning, uploading, and distribution of this book without permission is a theft of the author's intellectual property. If you would like permission to use material from the book (other than for review purposes), please contact kpgaines@outlook.com. Thank you for your support of author's rights.

All rights reserved.

ISBN: 979-8-9879003-0-7

DEDICATION

I dedicate this book to all the godly women that have passed through my life and left an example of what a godly woman is supposed to look like. But there is one in particularly that I want to point out—Kim Johnson, you touched my life in ways that you will never know. You are an amazing person and a sweet woman of God. Thank you for befriending me and being a great encouragement.

CONTENTS

	Acknowledgments	I
1	Introduction	1
2	Stop Comparing	9
3	God's Opinion-Not Others	24
4	Peace Makers-No Breaker	34
5	Self-Restraint	42
6	Slow Down	50
7	Show Goodness	56
8	Are You Faithful	62
9	Meekness Is Not Weak	67
10	Self-Control	73
11	Final Thoughts	80
12	Study Questions	86

ACKNOWLEDGMENTS

First and foremost, I thank Jesus Christ my savior for the gift of salvation that was given to me freely. If it weren't for His love and mercy, I wouldn't be here today. Many thanks to my family and friends that keep pushing me to write, if it weren't for them, this book would probably still be just a thought. To my husband, Kevin, thank you for supplying me with a place I can go and be alone to write, I love my new office! Kiara, my sweet daughter, thank you for continuing to be a sounding board for my ideas and helping me come up with new ones. To my son, Preston, thanks for helping me with all my computer issues…without you I'd be lost in the sea of technology. And at last, I can never forget to thank all the people who continue to doubt and try to convince me it's not possible, (even on book three), you all keep proving Philippians 4:13 true repeatedly…

I can do all things through Christ who strengthened me.

Introduction

Therefore, if any *woman* be in Christ, *she* is a new creature: old things are passed away; behold all things are new.

2 Corinthians 5:17
(*Author's Paraphrase*)

I'm Sorry

Fake friends are like the lights on a suicide bridge,
they can see that you are walking down the middle,
They see you stand on the edge, and they will see you
fall, but act like it's your fault that you are gone.

They will say they didn't see the signs,
but they did, they saw that you were wearing long
sleeves in the summer, pale skin, and red eyes.

They saw that the smile didn't quite meet the eyes.
All they cared for was that you were there for their
problems, but when you needed them, they were gone,
nowhere to be found.

You're the one that kept your head up—you're
the one that was there for you.
till…you couldn't take it anymore and let go.

I'm sorry if this is you, I'm sorry for the pain
they put you through. I'm sorry that they didn't
notice you slowly push them away. and I'm sorry to me
for being the 'you' in this poem.

I'm sorry for drawing on skin not with a pen—but a
blade. I am most sorry for putting myself in
this dark place—I'm sorry.
By: Kiara Espinoza

Are you a woman of God? Have you ever stopped to think about what that really means? Everywhere you go, you hear people say, *'I know who God is.'* When you open your Bible, you read about Him. When you go to church, you hear about Him. But do you really *know* Him? Does Christ live in you and through you? Have you let Him have complete control of your being? Do His attributes shine out to the world?

As you ponder these questions, I want to give you an insight into what this book is about; Galatians 5 tells us that to live holy, we must have His Spirit dwelling within us, and that Spirit must be leading us. And if the Spirit leads us, then the fruit of the Spirit should be evident in our life. What is the fruit of the Spirit? Galatians 5: 22-23 says: *But the fruit of the Spirit is love, joy, peace, longsuffering, gentleness, goodness, faith, meekness, temperance: against such, there is no law.* We will look at what these should look like in a godly woman's life. But first, let's look at what should not be found in a godly woman.

My daughter wrote the poem above. She was only 15 years old when she wrote those words. There were people in her life that made her feel she would never be enough. Most of the poems in this book were written by her during a very dark time. People in her life had made her feel worthless, broken, and inadequate. She felt she would never be as perfect as those around her. When she compared herself to these people that were trying to break her, she just didn't measure up.

How many times have you felt like you were inadequate when compared to others around you? Now answer this question—why are you comparing yourself with others? Did God call you to be like other people? No, He did not. He called you to be you and me to be me. We spend most of our lifetime beating ourselves up because we feel we're not pretty enough, tall enough, skinny enough, or we are too tall, too thin, or we're not smart enough, or we can't do something as well as someone else. The list goes on and on.

God wants us to look inside ourselves and see who He says we are. We can only find our true identity in Christ. And we must search out what that identity is. We are utterly incapable of loving anyone else when we are busy comparing ourselves to others and feeling that we don't measure up. This thinking only leads to destruction.

If you don't believe this is true, pay attention the next time you talk with a friend. See if you hear things like: *'She thinks she's all that—but she's not,'* or maybe something like: *'She thinks she is the best singer in church—but I don't like the way she sings,"* How about, *'She would be prettier if she'd lose a little weight,'* that could be said, *'She'd be prettier if she weren't so skinny—she looks sick.'*

In the Bible, this is referred to as *backbiting*. There are many verses on this subject in the Bible, but here are a few:

- Proverbs 16:28—A froward man soweth strife: and a whisperer separateth chief friends.
- Matthew 7:1-2—Judge not, that ye be not judged. For with what judgment ye judge, ye shall be judged: and with what measure ye mete, it shall be measured to you again.
- Proverbs 25:23—The north wind driveth away rain: so doth an angry countenance a backbiting tongue.

As a woman of God, trying to tear other people down should not be part of our repertoire. Instead, we should build people up, encourage them, and strengthen them. We should *be in behavior that becometh holiness, not false accusers, not given to much wine, teachers of good things* (Titus 2:3). To accomplish this, we must think like Christ. How do we do this? First, we must put on the mind of Christ (Philippians 2). Once we study to be like Christ and think like Him, then we won't have the desire to hurt others.

Now let's look at the other side of the coin. What if you are the one who such actions have hurt? You walk away with your head held high, knowing that other people's opinion doesn't define who you are. You don't retaliate; you don't start spreading negative things about the abuser. You walk away. Why? Because the negative things people say about you are not about you—it's about them.

It took my daughter a while to understand this point. From the beginning of her life, I had told her not to listen to other people's judgment of her. But in her words—there were so many people coming at her from every angle that she started believing them. The sad part is that several of the people who hurt her were family and claimed to be Christians.

Godly women don't go around spreading lies or nitpicking someone apart. Women who do this have forgotten who they are in Christ. Somewhere along the line, they stopped thinking like Christ. They let Satan convince them they are not good enough, smart enough, pretty enough, etc. So, when they see the people who have the attributes of Christ and see what is missing in themselves, they try to excuse their flaws by pointing out or creating deficiencies in others.

So why not just fix the problem—right? Satan has that blocked. He is now in their mind telling them that they will never measure up, and these women believe him. That is why we don't retaliate. Instead, we show them love and uplift them in prayer. Because when we punish—we have now given him power over us too. John 10 refers to Satan as a thief; and says he came to steal, kill and destroy. However, Christ came so that we may have life and have it more abundantly. As Godly women, we should guide people into that life, not push them out.

I'm thankful to say that today my daughter is 18. She is becoming an extraordinary woman seeking the heart of Christ. She devotes her time to helping me in this ministry and seeing other women grow in Christ. Don't be the reason people want to commit suicide, don't be the reason people are harming themselves. Don't be the reason someone is hurting.

If you are reading these words and think—I am that woman. I find myself saying terrible things about people to villainize them to others. This book is for you too. We are all guilty of this at some point in our lives. I know I am. As women, it is so easy to feel inadequate. The world around us has put out images of what the perfect woman is supposed to be, and when we don't measure up, it brings on these feelings of inadequacy. However, the worldly image is not what we should be chasing. Instead, we should read our Bible and fervently pray to be what Christ wants us to be.

God created each human being to be unique. He doesn't need two of anybody. We are designed in His fashion, after His likeness, to do the work He called us to do, the way He wants us to. Never will you find in the Bible Christ saying that we had to look a certain way, sing on perfect pitch, or do our service to Him perfectly. Beauty fades, and sometimes our voice will not cooperate when we try to hit that high note, and sometimes when we try to witness the words come out all jumbled. All that matters is that we are giving Him the best we have at that moment.

He's not up there taking notes every time you mispronounce a word when trying to read the Bible. Or if you woke up with your hair all a mess and it won't lay just right. Or if your voice crackled while you were singing in the choir. He only saw you being faithful to Him and giving Him your best effort. As Christians, we shouldn't judge people on these things, either. Instead, we should show the attributes of the fruit of the Spirit.

As you go through the chapters of this book, we will look at each attribute and dissect it so we can get a clear view of what that should look like in our life. At the end of each chapter, I have included a worksheet to brainstorm and write out areas that need work. I hope you enjoy the journey to becoming a perfectly imperfect woman of God.

Stop Comparing

And now abideth faith, hope, charity (love), these three; but the greatest of these is charity (love).

1 Corinthians 13:13

Perfectly Imperfect

Someone's always thinner,
Someone's always smarter,
Some have the most perfect lives,
While some have to try a little harder.
Some are so beautiful that
people stop and stare,
While there's some not so blessed-
with such a beauty rare.
Some are too thin,
Some are too tall,
While the short ones seem to be
the parody of them all.
Truth is- it's all an illusion,
We all have our imperfections.
But our worth is so much more
than what's seen in mirrored reflections.
So don't judge yourself so harshly,
nor others just the same,
We're all perfectly imperfect,
So go and state your claim.

By: Karen Gaines & Kiara Espinoza

We, as women, have been conditioned to compare ourselves to others in almost every facet of society. This conditioning stems from culture pushing the idea that a woman's worth depends on her physical beauty. It's the one thing that is consistently focused on; turn on your television or pick up a magazine, and you will see clearly what I mean. Society paints this picture that this is how a beautiful woman should look.

While you are over there wishing you could be that beautiful, stop and realize that the person in that picture wishes she was that flawless too. Most of what you see is edited to show perfections that don't exist. As women, we torment ourselves because we don't measure up to what society wants. Stop keeping score!

When we compare ourselves to others, we allow them to drive our behavior; often, it is destructive. This destruction is focused inwardly on yourselves or outwardly on others. Or both. Either way, it all starts with inadequate feelings toward yourself. You focus your energy on bringing others down instead of raising yourself. When left unresolved, feelings of inadequacy too often turn to self-harm.

Comparing yourself to others makes you feel insecure about who you are. Focusing on the parts of yourself that you feel self-conscious about only results in feeling that you're not good enough, you don't get approval from everyone, and you don't feel confident in yourself. Repeatedly looking at others to determine how things should play out in your life only heightens when you think you don't measure up. You then find yourself wallowing in this negative energy, and before you know it, you will transfer this onto others.

You began to point out other people's flaws to make yourself feel better. Too often, this stems from the fact that we see something in them that we want to change about ourselves. As a woman of God, we should uplift one another, not tear each other down. The only way to do this is to see you as God sees you. Psalm 139:14 says, *I will praise thee; for I am fearfully and wonderfully made: Marvellous are thy works; And that my soul knoweth right well.* God doesn't make mistakes. You are who He intended you to be. So, embrace you and stop comparing yourself to others.

When we embrace our differences and realize that each of us is who God wants us to be, we will begin to lift each other and encourage the ones that haven't quite gotten there yet. Comparing yourself to others all the time is choosing to be unhappy. Because the truth is, there will always be someone better than you, prettier than you, more intelligent than you, thinner than you; when that is what you are focused on constantly, you are letting it rob you of your peace, joy, and happiness.

Philippians 4:11 tell us, *Not that I speak in respect of want: for I have learned, in whatsoever state I am, therewith be content.*

Shifting your focus to what God has given or is going to give helps you realize that you are what and where God wants you at this moment. While you may not be where you want to be, take time to see how far you have come. Take time to see how God has blessed you and wonderfully created you to be what He wanted. Doing this will add to your happiness and takes your focus off other people and more on being who He wants you to be.

So far, we have focused on how comparing causes destructive jealousy to rise against others. Let's talk now about when we turn the destruction in on ourselves. We tend to isolate ourselves from others. We can't let ourselves love and be loved. We find ourselves in a miserable state of mind. Depression creeps in; we feel alone, lost, and worthless. Many turn to drugs and alcohol, meaningless sexual relationships, or cutting, burning or biting themselves. Some are trying to numb, while others are trying to feel. Both sides are choosing destructive behaviors and self-harm to medicate.

Look inside you and realize that the person you are comparing yourself to—they have insecurities too. If self-harm is caused by someone who chose to point out your deficiencies—know that it's because they have them too. Their harsh behavior had nothing to do with you—it's all about them.

God made us all unique, not so we could compare ourselves, but that we would all use what He gave us to join together and glorify Him. Learn to love what makes us all different. Doing so will benefit you in the long run. Comparing yourself to others will only harm you. You will have a negative attitude as you place unrealistic expectations on yourself. Embrace you—love you because only you can be you, and there's nothing wrong with that.

Love

Now, let's talk about love.

Love is a word that gets thrown around a lot. I love going to the mountains or the beach. I love my car. I love chocolate. I love dogs and cats. However, this is more to the extreme of desires than real authentic love. So, what is real love, and how do we obtain it? If you google the definition of love, you get primarily- *an intense feeling of deep affection.* And-A *great interest and pleasure in something.* Although these are not wrong, love goes much deeper than these meanings.

The love Galatians speaks about as an attribute of the fruit of the Spirit is more on godly love. This love is the fatherly love of God for humans and the reciprocal human love for God. In the Bible, transcendent agape love is the highest form of love and is in contrast to all other types of love. God first shows this in John 3:16: *For God so loved the world that He gave His only begotten Son, that whosoever believeth in Him should not perish, but have everlasting life.* He sent His Son for the world's redemption. Jesus later proved this love on the cross as He gave His life so we could all have life. However, it didn't end there with Him. He arose on the third day so we, too, could access this incredible love.

You may be asking what this love looks like in your life. How do I love like Jesus? First, you must accept Him and His will into your heart. When you first come to utterly love Him, you then love like Him. The Bible gives us an example of this love in 1 Corinthians 13. Paul writes: *Though I speak with the tongue of men and of angels, and have not charity (love), I am become as a sounding brass, or a tinkling cymbal. And though I have the gift of prophecy, and understand all mysteries, and all knowledge; and though I have all faith, so that I could remove mountains, and have not charity (love), I am nothing. And though I bestow all my goods to feed the poor, and though I give my body to be burned, and have not charity (love), it profiteth me nothing.*

What is he saying here? He's saying that it doesn't matter what he has or what he does; if it's not done in love, it is a waste of time. To break that down more— Paul could be a great speaker, sharing wisdom and knowledge with everyone he meets; he could give to every charity there is out there; he could be perfect in everything he sets out to do, but if it's not done in love through Christ, it profits him nothing. The only way to experience this love is through Jesus Christ.

Once we love Him wholeheartedly, He will then show us how to love ourselves so we can love others. Wait, love ourselves? Now that's a hard one. How can I love myself when one eyelid droops lower than the other and my nose is crooked from being broken? How can I love myself when I'm not at the perfect weight? And look at those crow's feet sprouting around my eyes. Whatever yours is, we all have those imperfections that make us feel as if we don't measure up. For this one, we are going to look at 1 Samuel 16:7. The second part of this verse tells us: *For the Lord seeth not as man seeth; for man looketh on the outward appearance, but the Lord looketh on the heart.* So, what kind of person are you in your heart? That is where true beauty is found.

We will never love ourselves when we base love on what we see, touch, or feel. Tangible things will never bring us happiness within ourselves. When we learn to love what we can't see about ourselves—despite what we see—we can look for the same in others and not what is on the outside. In other words, we love them despite what we see that may not be so appealing to us. We no longer view them as competition. Instead, we see them as Jesus does- someone with the exact wants and desires we have. We see them as someone who needs love, compassion, understanding, acceptance, and, most of all, the redemption power of salvation through Jesus Christ.

However, some are harder than others. You may run across one that hasn't yet learned to accept who God created them to be. They may be cold and bitter because their life hasn't been good. These are the ones who need to see the love of Christ shining through you the most. It's not up to you to change them. Don't even give negative feedback to them. Remember what I said at the beginning of this chapter? What people say about you is not about you. Just keep smiling and tell them that you are sorry that they feel so low about themselves that they need to tear down others. Then, ensure that Jesus loves them, and so do you—then walk away. Plant the seed of love everywhere you go.

Love is the most important of the attributes of the fruit of the Spirit. It takes love to have all the rest. As I close this chapter, consider the paraphrased verses below. Change the love to your name and see how many fit in your life. If there are any that don't, that is an area you need to work on before you can love like Christ.

(1 Corinthians 14:4-8 Author's paraphrase and thoughts)

- Love is patient- God doesn't just love you on the good days and despises you on your worst. His passion doesn't ebb and flow, with Monday blahs and weekend euphoria. Instead, His love is patient and unfailing through health and sickness, anger and sorrow, triumph and failure. Our love for one another should echo His. Patience isn't just a virtue. It's at the heart of what real love is all about.
- Love is kind- Kindness isn't a manipulative effort to get what we want. Instead, it's giving something without the hope of reward. God loves us and blesses us continually, though there's

nothing we could ever give back to Him. He doesn't need anything, but He still shows kindness—even to those who refuse to love Him back.

- Love does not envy- God warned us so sternly about envy and wanting what others have in Exodus 20:17. This is because He is the one who takes care of us.

When we envy, we're showing our dissatisfaction with what He's provided for us, our desire to have more than He's planned. Envy rots away the connections between us. We want something we feel we deserve. Our frustration grows and grows while our love shrinks. However, when we put away envy, we're left with a love for humanity that grows fresh every day. Why? Because we are content with what God has given us. When we are looking for the best in another person, when we're on the hunt for the good in them and not wanting what they have—we don't feel the need to tear them down.

- Love does not boast; it is not proud- Boast means to brag or point to oneself. Boasting is not a symbol of love. Love does not boast simply because love is focused on others outside of yourself. Someone who boasts is full of themselves, magnifying their accomplishments and too occupied with themselves to notice others. Love turns the perspective outward. A person with God's love will uplift others, focus on their needs, and offer help without the thought of repayment or recognition. Christian love is not proud or focus on self. Pride and boasting cannot coexist with godly love.

- Love does not dishonor others. It is not self-seeking- In other words—love does not abuse others. Love does not manipulate others toward self-centered ways and means. Love does not make someone do something. Love affirms and encourages, but it isn't pushy to forcefully get its own way. Love isn't pushy with words, either. It honors the fact that each person and their decisions are their own to make. When someone is wrong or headed down the wrong path in life, we can tell them with truth and love, but we can't scream and yell or demand them by force just because that is what we want for them. The second part of this is *love is not self-seeking*. What this is saying is it's not *me first*. Matthew 6:33 tells us *seek ye first the kingdom of God and His righteousness, and all these things will be added unto you.* That's how we become full of God's love. We trust Him to care for us so we can take care of the things God wants us to. We love others, and we seek their good. We pursue things that bless others; we put them first because love isn't about "me-first."
- Love is not easily angered- 2 Peter 3:9 highlights God's love for the world. *He is patient with you, not wanting anyone to perish, but everyone to come to repentance.* We should be the same towards others. Being easily angered usually

involves making snap judgments, seeking instant payback, and refusing to grant second chances. However, true love refuses to jump to conclusions, take revenge, or hastily judge anyone.
- Love keeps no record of wrongs- Jesus provides the ultimate example of this type of love. On the cross, He paid the price for the entire world's sins. While we were still sinners—Christ died for us. Yet, He keeps no record of our wrongs once we are forgiven. So often, people say they love each other, but as soon as one gets angry, the list of past sins comes out! Accusations fly, painful memories are dredged up, and bygones are no longer bygones. That is not love. True, godly love forgives and refuses to keep track of personal slights received. The focus of love is not one's own pain but the needs of the loved one. We should not allow people to continue hurting or abusing others. That is not what this is telling us. The goal is to have a spirit of reconciliation, forgive those who seek forgiveness, and let the past stay in the past.
- Love does not delight in evil but rejoices with the truth- True godly love rejoices in what is right and good. Anything that covers up sin or seeks to justify wrongdoing is the polar opposite of godly love. Love does not sweep it under the rug. Love does not try to find ways to get away with bad behavior and promotes virtue. True godly love

has nothing to hide. Further, to *not delight in evil* carries the idea of not gloating over someone else's guilt. It is common for people to rejoice when a person is found guilty of a crime or caught in a sin; this is not love. Love rejoices in the virtue of others, not in their vices. Sin is an occasion for sorrow, not for joy. The better we understand godly love, the more we will sorrow over those who sin. The more we love the truth, the better we can love those around us.

- Love always protects- one of the marks of godly love is that it always seeks to protect other people; this does not mean that we excuse wrongdoing or seek to evade the natural consequences of sin; it means that we strengthen what is weak, shield what is vulnerable, and forgive what is provoking.
- Love always trusts- A person with God's love will always trust. That is, this person will not be suspicious of the ones they love. To trust someone means that you are ever ready to believe the best. A person may have a checkered past or be in some other way undeserving of trust, yet godly love is able to look past that and meet the need of the individual. Mistrust, caginess, and suspicion are at odds with godly love.
- Love always hopes- The hope within us is Christ. If He lives within us, His hope is seen in how we treat others. Living with such an attitude reflects the ways of Christ, leads to holy living, and

brings glory to the heavenly Father. Part of showing love is hoping, and part of hoping is seeing the potential of others. In love, we can always be hopeful and show confidence in others. A positive attitude's impact on another person's life is immeasurable. Peter failed Jesus, yet the Lord restored him. The Corinthians failed Paul in some ways, yet the apostle, in love, patiently corrected them and sanctified them. Love always points to a brighter day ahead. Love is the lifeline that the hurting can hold. As long as there is love, there will be hope.

- Love always perseveres- There is persistence to love, even in tough times. Love doesn't quit or give up. Godly love is not a fleeting romance type of love or a fading feeling. Instead, godly love perseveres during the good times and bad; a godly person's love will endure life's challenges and remain steadfast. A person with godly love will consistently seek what is best for others. Godly love isn't on again, off again; it is a commitment to always seek the highest good, no matter what adversity befalls.

As I mentioned, love is essential to becoming a perfectly imperfect woman of God. He doesn't care about your physical flaws or how well you sing or play an instrument. Nor does He care about how many pimples you have or if your hair looks perfect today. He only cares about what is in your heart and how you treat others. So, learn to love like Christ, and you'll find the true beauty within you; then, you can find it in others.

Thought to Ponder

God's Opinion—Not Others

And ye now therefore have sorrow: but I will see you again, and your heart shall rejoice, and your joy no man taketh from you.
John 16:22

Chains

I want to be happy,
I want to be free.
But these chains
they won't shake from me.
I want to spread my wings and fly
And feel pure happiness deep inside.
Asking for help
but been denied,
So, these cold steel chains
keep me locked inside.
I lay awake
And cannot sleep,
Wondering sincerely,
Why am I so weak?
These chains were placed
By other hands,
Their opinion of me
Caused these bands.
To free myself,
I must realize,
What others think of me must count as lies.

By: Kiara Espinoza

We just looked at what comparing ourselves to others can do. Now let's go a little deeper into what happens when we get locked into destructive behavior. If we are not careful, they become joy snatchers. A friend of mine once said, "If I didn't care so much—I could be happy." That statement runs into the deep crevices of a woman's mind. If my parents didn't hurt me, if I wasn't molested as a child, if I weren't ever cheated on, if I were never bullied, if I were never abused, if I had of went to college, if I had a better life, if I—on and on.

But you were. However, that's not who you are—unless you let it be. I can hear your thoughts—*easy for you to say. You sit behind a computer and type out words—your research probably came from a book or online.* No. My research came from life. And for many years, I let those things define me. I let people convince me that I was worthless. Yeah, someone once told me that I wasn't pretty enough. Some came right out and said I was ugly. When I was nine years old, a little girl looked me right in the eyes and said, "No one likes you, you know—why are you even still alive." This little girl was a few years younger than I was. These were such harsh words for such a young girl. And that's only one, and there were many.

I grew up and became a woman who still believed those lies. I believed them so much that I stayed in destructive and abusive relationships because I felt I deserved it. Yeah, you read that right. Like my daughter's poem at the beginning of this chapter—I let those chains keep me bound in hopeless despair. I couldn't break free, no matter how hard I tried. I'd end a relationship only to start a new one that soon mirrored the one before it.

Why was this happening?
Am I that bad?
Am I really that unlovable?
Why am I alive?
Should I end it?

I was really caught up in believing all the things I had ever been told. The negative drowned out what my parents told me. They were the only ones who seemed to see the good—or did they? Maybe they were saying what they felt they had to as parents.

I stayed in this shackled way of thinking until I was in my thirties. That's sad—but oh so true. When my kid's dad and I split, I decided I wasn't doing it anymore. I spent three years focusing on my brokenness. I discovered that I had spent more time worrying about what other people thought of me than what God's thoughts were towards me. Jeremiah 29: 11-13 says, *For I know the thoughts that I think towards you, saith the Lord, thoughts of peace, and not of evil, to give you an expected end.* And then we turn to Romans 5:8, which says, *But God commanded his love toward us, that, while we were yet sinners, Christ died for us.* Wow! Even in my ugliest sin—God still considered me lovable! Can you imagine that? And He does you too.

Don't let *joy snatchers* rob you of who you are in

Christ! However, don't find yourself on the side of being the one who steals someone's joy, either. Before speaking evil or degrading of someone, ask yourself why you feel the need to tear someone down. What is lacking in you? Where have you believed others over God? Because women of God don't go around tearing others down—we lift them and build them up.

Joy

When you look up joy, you find words like happiness, elation, and excitement. So often, people today think that pursuing pleasure means trying to find what will make them happy. But let's look at the verses in of Habakkuk chapter one. In this book, Habakkuk is troubled by what he sees happening in the world around him. Just like the world we live in today, he saw difficulties, trials, hardships, setbacks, violence, crime, suffering, tribulations, and disappointments. He was so disturbed that he prayed in Habakkuk 1:2, *'O Lord, how long shall I cry out to you for help but you will not hear! Even cry out unto thee of violence, and thou wilt not save?'*

Habakkuk was troubled because of what he knew to be true concerning God's character (His justice and holiness), and the things he saw (injustice and sin) seemed to co-exist as if they were meant to be together.

Finally, God gave him his answer in chapter 2, verses 3 and 4—*And the Lord answered me, and said, write the vision, and make it plain upon the tables, that he may run that readeth it. For the vision is yet for an appointed time, but at the end it shall speak, and not lie: though it tarry, wait for it; because it will surely come, it will not tarry. Behold, his soul which is lifted up is not upright in him: but the just shall live by his faith.* Habakkuk had discovered that God was not indifferent to the suffering of His people. Still, he understood that God had appointed a glorious time when He would save His people from their sins, rescue them from their enemies and wipe away every tear from their eyes.

In Habakkuk's day, things were to get worse before they got better, and he was called to live by faith—to trust God, who is faithful to rescue His people and true to His word. As we read further in Habakkuk 3:19, he states, '*The Lord God is my strength, and he will make my feet like hinds feet, and he will make me to walk upon mine high places.* Hinds refers to graceful, swift, and sure-footed deer that can climb rocky cliffs and never stumble or fall.

Habakkuk makes two monumental statements that I want you to remember. He said, '*...the just shall live by faith.*' and '*The Lord God is my Strength; He will make my feet like deer's feet, and He will make me walk in high places.*' (paraphrased). Habakkuk is describing his sure-footed reliance on God. He realized that he only needed to have faith in God.

God wants us to come to the realization and assurance that Habakkuk came to—that He is our sovereign strength and will enable us to walk over the hills and mountains in our lives. The transformation of our human feet to deer's feet (spiritually speaking) takes place when we begin to see, trust, and rely on the never-failing character of God to bring us through all that life can bring our way.

Let's look deeper at what deer's feet represent. A deer's feet are designed for climbing up high hills and mountains with ease. God wants us to learn to trust Him no matter what we face because this verse tells us that as long as we trust Him, He will get us through it. He'll make our feet like deer feet so that we can easily maneuver any rough terrain that life brings our way. When the bills are due, and money is short, we know He's got us. He fights for us when people come against us and try to tarnish our name. When sickness comes, and there's nothing the doctors can do, He heals us. In times like these, He makes our feet like hinds' feet so that we make it over every obstacle.

I hear you asking: "What does all this have to do with joy?" The joy we are talking about as an attribute of the fruit of the Spirit has a meaning of calm delight or inner gladness. It means to rejoice because of grace. Godly joy is not based on our possessions or circumstances. This joy means inward peace and soundness that is not affected by what is happening around us. Romans 5:3-5 tells us, *And not only so, but we glory in tribulations also: knowing that tribulation worketh patience; and patience, experience; and experience hope: and hope maketh not ashamed; because the love of God is shed abroad in our hearts by the Holy Ghost which is given to us.* Glory in tribulations?

The answer to that is straightforward. As a woman of God, we are not contingent on circumstances. We never say, 'I could have joy if___.' Our joy comes not from what we have, but instead, it comes from *what* we are. It doesn't come from where we are; it comes from *whose* we are. Joy isn't dependent on what brings us happiness; it comes from knowing *who is in control,* even when faced with undesirable circumstances. There is joy in the world, but it is hollow and fleeting. However, the joy that comes from God always brings contentment and is everlasting.

The joy I'm talking about has nothing to do with the euphoria that comes when something good happens to us. It is a choice we make every day. Philippians 4:4 tell us, *Rejoice in the Lord always; again I say, rejoice.* 1 Thessalonians 5:16 tell us to *Rejoice always.* One of my favorite verses we find in James chapter 1 is, *My brethren, count it all joy when ye fall into divers temptations; knowing this, that the trying of your faith worketh patience. But let patience have her perfect work, that ye may be perfect and entire, wanting nothing.* Contentment. That one word sums it up.

When we can be content with what God is doing, we can move forward in joy. If we never faced hardships or pain, we'd never know God would deliver us from them all. We'd never know His healing power if we never faced sickness; we'd never know of His miraculous abilities if we were never in situations that only He can fix. After all, He never promised that life wouldn't be hard. He promises never to leave us nor forsake us. (Hebrews 13:5, Let your conversation be without covetousness; and be content with such things as you have: for he hath said, I will never leave thee, nor forsake thee.)

Joy can't be found looking at what others have and feeling as though you have been cheated; this can be material things like houses, cars, and money, or this can be wishing you were skinny like someone or had brown eyes instead of blue or any other thing that causes you to envy and takes your eyes off what God has blessed you with, or what He is doing in your life. Doing this zaps our joy; now we feel cheated as if God loves these more than us. When you take your eyes off what God is doing in you and your life, you let go of the joy of knowing that He has you right where He wants you. Realizing where He wants you is the best place to be, even if it's in the middle of a life storm, is what brings perfect joy.

Do you see how joy is related to love in the previous chapter? With love, you must learn God's way of loving yourself unconditionally, the way He loves you; once you get that right, you can love other people unconditionally. Joy is the same. When you realize that God is *working things for your good* (Romans 8:28), you then can find joy in knowing that everything will work out the way it should—for your good.

To sum it up: godly joy is the delighted response of Christians to the fact that we have been given a precious truth, gift, and understanding of a way of life that brings fulfillment—now and forever. When we consider and genuinely believe the amazing truth of the Kingdom of God and our part in it, how can we not be purely joyful in every aspect of our lives? So smile! Don't let anything or anyone steal your God-given joy!

Thoughts to Ponder

Peace Makers—Not Breakers

Be careful for nothing; but in every thing by prayer and supplication with thanksgiving let your requests be made known unto God. And the peace of God, which passeth all understanding, shall keep your hearts and minds through Christ Jesus.
Philippians 4:6-7

The Clouds

How is that so?
It's like they are sitting on some type of force,
Like if the force gives way,
they will clasp to the ground with a thud.
They seem angry at times,
But by others they seem soft and gentle,
small, big, mean, and kind.
No matter what they look like
They are one thing—clouds.
That's the same for you and me.
We may look mean, kind, small, buff,
chubby, skinny, or by what you wear.
Either way—we are people.
Yes, we are different.
But you don't have to point out others flaws.
I am me and you are you,
Love yourself like no tomorrow
Embrace being perfectly imperfect.
By Kiara Espinoza

Peacemakers don't go around stirring up dirt on people. I like to think of peace breakers as adult bullies. (Yeah, they exist.) We see them everywhere—most of the time, these adults are behind the little bullies at school. Kids learn what they live.

If daddy is always calling mommy names, then little Johnny thinks it's okay when he does it to the other kids at school. But, if mommy is always making fun of overweight people or using derogatory names to describe the trashy woman in the parking lot at Walmart, then little Sarah is going to think she can do the same to the overweight kids at school. That little girl she deems prettier than she is has to be trash, or she wouldn't be that pretty.

You may wonder why I chose the poem above for a peace chapter. First, look closely at the way she describes the clouds. I look at storm clouds, and I'm one of those that see anger. They are dark and scary as they roll in. However, a friend of mine once described them as dark, fluffy pillows illuminating the lightning bolts like beautiful tapestries in the sky. I had never thought to look at them that way. But I looked at them differently once she pointed it out to me.

Wouldn't it be nice to see that about each other? People are the same. We are all different. What if we looked at those differences in how we view the clouds?

What if we realized that when we take all our differences and put them together, we create a beautiful masterpiece to fit together in harmony? I like to think of it as a church choir. I can't sing soprano, but my alto joins perfectly with your high pitch. Then someone comes along with a perfect tenor voice. Together we make beautiful music.

My point is—don't focus on what you can't do or can. Or what someone else has that you don't. Focus on how we can join it together to make perfect harmony. That's how we live in peace. So often, we find ourselves in a storm where we feel we are going under—peace isn't there. We fight anxiety, depression, and hopelessness. Where is your focus? Is it based on what you have, or don't have to weather the storm? Or is it on Christ?

When we focus on Christ, we look at the storm clouds differently. We see beauty amid the storm and not all the ugliness around us. We then try to help those around us find that beauty in themselves instead of comparing their white fluffy clouds to our dark stormy ones and then trying to bring them into the storm with us. We instead embrace the place that God has each of us, knowing that together we can weather any storm.

Peace

Peace. Just saying the word brings a feeling of euphoria to our souls. But what does it mean exactly? First, of course, one of the greatest human desires is for peace: peace between nations, peace between neighbors, and peace within our own minds. Yet our experience confirms the biblical assessment: "The way of peace they have not known" (Romans 3:17; quoted from Isaiah 59:8).

Acting in a way that leads to true and lasting peace is not part of our natural human tendencies. Instead, the apostle Paul wrote that our human nature leads to "hatred, contentions, jealousies, outbursts of wrath, selfish ambitions, dissensions ... murders" (Galatians 5:20-21). In contrast, those who receive God can access a new nature that allows us to grow in the fruit of peace (verse 22).

Peace is the opposite of James 4:1-4, which describes the cause of war. *"From whence come wars and fightings among you? come they not hence, even of your lusts that war in your members? Ye lust, and have not: ye kill, and desire to have, and cannot obtain: ye fight and war, yet ye have not, because ye ask not. Ye ask, and receive not, because ye ask amiss, that ye may consume it upon your lusts. Ye adulterers and adulteresses, know ye not that the friendship of the world is enmity with God? whosoever therefore will be a friend of the world is the enemy of God."*

Notice Philippians 4:6-7: *Be careful for nothing; but in every thing by prayer and supplication with thanksgiving let your requests be made known unto God. And the peace of God, which passeth all understanding, shall keep your hearts and minds through Christ Jesus.* God's perfect peace is one of those wonderfully deep things of God that have not "entered into the heart of man" but are only "spiritually discerned" (1 Corinthians 2:9, 14). The fruit of the Spirit of peace provides the inner peace of mind and contentment found only by living God's way of life—even in less-than-peaceful situations.

So, how do we demonstrate peace? First, we must practice the way of peace, starting in the only area we can affect- our sphere of influence. Remember, Paul urged us "if it is possible" and "as much as depends on you" to live peaceably with "all men," this will be challenging. Here are a few ideas:

- Drop conversations that are getting out of hand; this might involve saying something like: "Let's agree to disagree." Then be satisfied that you can't change someone else's mind about certain things. Peace is knowing that God's intervention might be necessary to change someone's thinking (including our own).
- Make yourself stand out as the calm and collected one in whatever encounters you experience. Others may fight or say insulting, jealous, or prideful things, but we should edify, build up and walk away from an encounter if necessary.
- Respect other human beings as potential future members of the family of God. Remember that God does not want anyone to perish (2 Peter 3:9), no matter how angry you are at the person.
- Don't be concerned about things others say about you or do to you. Not only does this zap your

joy—it causes contention and strife between you and others, and what are the results? It also takes your peace.

Think about the times you may be anxious, frustrated, or chaotic. The world may seem to be spinning around 100 miles per hour, and you need a moment to sit and be still. The overwhelming peace that can comfort you during this time comes from having Christ within us. Peace is knowing that our God is in control.

Just like we, as Christian women, are called to be peacemakers, there is also a peace that you can have in every situation that life throws your way. *That peace that surpasses all understanding* is ever present in every situation you face. It could be us having to be the peacemakers and having to keep our anger in check. Or it could be holding your tongue when those hurtful thoughts of another person tempt to come out of your mouth. It can also be knowing that God is always in control of everything, and everything will be alright, no matter how a situation looks.

You can have peace knowing God is working when the bills come in, and the money is not there. You may already be in a situation where the money didn't come, and now you must move out of your home and have no place to go—God is working on your behalf. You only have to be still and know that He is God. He said, *I will never leave you, nor forsake you.* You can rest in knowing that He is a God that cannot lie.

There will never be peace in this world. There will always be war, fighting, riots, and such, but you can have peace that is not of this world, nor can it be understood by the human brain. It can only be felt in the hearts of true believers of God. This peace only comes from relinquishing all of you entirely in the trusting hands of a living God.

The word *peace* appears nearly 429 times in the Bible; this tells us the importance of this attribute. Peace is listed in the top three characteristics of the fruit of the Spirit. The rest of the list is impossible without love, joy, and peace. But the greatest of these is love.

Thought to Ponder

_____

_____

_____

_____

_____

_____

_____

_____

Self-Restraint

9 The Lord is not slack concerning his promise, as some men count slackness; but is longsuffering to us-ward, not willing that any should perish, but that all should come to repentance.
                    2 Peter 3:9

Walls

I'm afraid you'll break down these walls of mine
That I've tried so hard to build,
I've tried to hide from your sight
But you seem to find me still.
Oh, curse this stupid heart of mine,
That wants to love but cannot find,
So, leave me be
For you cannot see
I was meant to be alone.

By: Kiara Espinoza

The poem on the opposite page was written at a very dark time in my daughter's life. She had been hurt so many times by people she had put her trust in that she no longer trusted herself to interact with anyone. She would later explain this to me as it seemed like the more she put her heart out there, the more it only got crushed. This continued for so long that she began to believe that she was meant to be alone—without family, friends, or acquaintances.

She was only 15 years old at this time. She wasn't adjusting well to those middle school years. We all know this is a rough time for many. But to give a little background, her dad walked out when she was four and never had anything to do with us through the years. As a mother, I tried hard to fill that void for my kids; it seemed to be working until I decided to move back to my hometown; this should have been a good move. It brought us closer to family and people we couldn't see often.

However, for my daughter, it meant moving away from the only people she ever knew. People who loved and cherished her were no longer in her life. I'm not saying that my family didn't love us, but my daughter hadn't grown up around them. We would visit on holidays and through the summer, but outside her grandparents, she didn't have a bond with the other family members. By the time she reached middle school, certain family members had begun to make her feel alienated and worthless.

Around this time, I discovered she was cutting. I was devastated. How could I have missed this? After a while, she would explain that she had numbed herself to all the hostile forces to the point that she started to cut to feel something. You may be asking—what does this have to do with self-restraint or longsuffering?

As a mother, I wanted to go to the people that had hurt her so deeply that she was doing this to herself and handle the matter myself! The thing was that these people never knew that she felt this way. She never confronted them. She pretended she didn't notice what they said or did. She hid it so well that even I didn't know she was hurting so badly. I practiced self-restraint when I didn't react; that would have worsened the problem for her. So I instead focused my attention on helping her to heal.

When we think about longsuffering, it covers many areas, such as self-restraint and, as some bible translations refer, patients. You can't have the "I'll fix it myself" mentality when you want to portray longsuffering the godly way. As women of God, we must be patient and let Him deal with these situations.

Longsuffering

Longsuffering is often defined as *suffering*

long. Although that is a good answer, a better definition is needed. In the Bible, the Greek words used translate to *long* and *tempered.* Giving us- *long-tempered.* To be considered longsuffering is to have self-restraint when stirred to anger. A longsuffering person does not have a short fuse but chooses not to retaliate or punish but patiently forbears. It is also associated with *mercy* and *hope.* A person with this fruit active in their life does not surrender to circumstances or succumb to trials.

How can we, as women of God, have longsuffering active in our lives? When we accept Christ in our hearts and study His word, we can then learn how to activate this fruit. It should come naturally, especially when we know the characteristics of God, because one of the first things we see is God's patience with sinners- with us! We should be grateful that God is the epitome of longsuffering. However, when we accept Jesus, we take on the very life of God and His divine nature.

Popular belief is that this means that a person is weak. However, this shows great strength in a person's character and boldness in resisting rash reactions. Just think how much better our lives would be if we practiced this more often. Instead, impatience, oversensitivity, intolerance, and impulsive anger seem to have taken over the world and our lives. In the news, we see it every day; people killing people over trivial things, parents murdering tiny babies and children, husbands killing wives- wives killing husbands- children killing parents, or someone getting shot or stabbed just because they looked at someone the wrong way. We all need to learn to practice longsuffering a little more.

The evil influence we all are infected with is our own selfish nature. Paul refers to our human nature as *the flesh* or selfish tendencies as *works of the flesh* (Galatians 5: 19-21). He describes these as hatred, contentions, jealousies, outburst of wrath, selfish ambitions, dissensions, heresies, envy, and murders (paraphrased). It's sad to say, but most people have let these things control them, and it is these that show a lack of longsuffering, a lack of knowledge of what God wants His children to be.

Most people these days tend to overreact to everything. They get defensive, interpret a remark as an attack, and then strike back. Are you one of those? So many people carry around a lot of inner anger from their past. With every small hurt or annoyance, this storehouse of anger keeps building and building—until the slightest provocation brings the offense to the surface and out into the open.

We tend to give many excuses for our anger. But the truth is, human anger is self-centered and sinful. James 1:20 tells us, *"For the wrath of man worketh not the righteousness of God."* Think of that before you react in anger. Longsuffering is shown through walking away or responding nicely to a rude remark made to you.

Although most people will never admit to hating anyone, you must remember that love and hate are action words, no matter what you say with your mouth. What messages are your actions showing? Love is expressed by helping people, and hate by harming them. Are you helping people or hurting them? If you want to make sure you portray Christ the way you should start guarding your thoughts and attitude. One thing to always remember is that it is our thoughts and mindset that feed our actions and words. (Luke 6:45 A good man out of the good treasure of his heart bringeth forth that which is good; and an evil man out of the evil treasure of his heart bringeth forth that which is evil: for of the abundance of the heart his mouth speaketh.)

If hate is what you have in your heart, no matter how much you say that you don't hate anyone—hate is what you will send out. So examine yourself with these questions: Am I motivated by love, respect, patience, and compassion, or am I motivated by resentment, contempt, intolerance, and hardness of heart?

Without God's gift of longsuffering, we fall short of what He wants us to be. The best way to practice this is through restraint and doing nothing. Always stop and ask: What does God want me to say or do? Then if you feel that something needs to be said, keep this closing verse in mind: Proverbs 15:1 A soft answer turneth away wrath: but grievous words stir up anger.

Thoughts to Ponder

_____

_____

Slow Down

Let brotherly love continue. Be not forgetful to entertain strangers: for thereby some have entertained angels unawares.
Hebrews 13:1-2

_____

If Only

Why did you rush on by today
As if I wasn't there?
Would it have hurt for you to stop a moment
And show me that you care?
A word of kindness
Would have been nice,
To prove these voices inside my head
Are just lies.
But those harsh words hurt
As you pushed me aside
It proved that I'm only scum
In other people's eyes,
So, as I sit here on the brink
Of choosing to take my last breath,
Do I choose a life of pain and hurt,
Or to close my eyes to death?
No one seems to care
If I live or die,
Why couldn't you have just been nice
As you passed me by.
By: Kiara Espinoza

The poem above is heartbreaking. Yet so many face this feeling every day. Some live to testify of the love that broke through and wouldn't let them do it. But so many don't. When my daughter was asked, in theory, what kept her from doing it, she replied that it was the thought of what it would do to her mama. The only person she knew, without a doubt, loved her unconditionally. I'm thankful that she chose me. Because in choosing me, she chose life. Today she is a woman of God working beside me in this ministry to help lead others to Christ.

We live in a ruthless world. Everybody is in a hurry to get to the top; they don't seem to care about how their words and actions affect other people. Yet, words and actions have a crucial impact on other people's lives. We need to slow down and think before we react. Get out of the 'Me' way of thinking and get back to the heart of Christ.

What would it hurt if we learned to smile at people? Sometimes that is all it takes to send a ray of hope to someone. When we realize that we are not our own, but we are bought with a price (1 Corinthians 3:23), we can then learn to act in love and gentleness the way our creator made us operate. And He created all of us. We all belong to Him. So, when we are rude, unloving, or complacent to someone, we do it to someone who belongs to Him. Everyone—sinner or saint, we all belong to Him. He created us all; He died for us all. So, think of that the next time you choose not to show love, kindness, or gentleness to someone.

Gentleness

When you look up gentleness, the definition given is—Mildness of manner or disposition. So the word gentleness is perfect for describing how someone acts when they are soft, calm, and sweet to other people.

As we have mentioned before, the fruit of the Spirit is essentially the character of Jesus. As women of God, we should have these characteristics active in our lives. Gentleness is a trait lacking in a lot of people today. The quality of gentleness is the opposite of harshness to others. It is power over one's Spirit that exudes a meek and mild person like Jesus. Let's look at James 3:16-18

For where envying and strife is, there is confusion and every evil work. But the wisdom that is from above is first pure, then peaceable, gentle, and easy to be intreated, full of mercy and good fruits, without partiality, and without hypocrisy. And the fruit of righteousness is sown in peace of them that make peace.

As becoming godly women, we should be peacemakers with all people. That means we respond in gentleness when someone is rude to us. Not retaliate in anger but show the love of Christ. What happens most often is that people view gentleness as weakness or passivity. True gentleness, however, is just the opposite. It requires great strength. Gentleness comes from a state of humility. Therefore, someone who lacks gentleness is often prideful and easily angered or feels the need for revenge.

Like the story I spoke about in the last chapter, I could have let my flesh overtake me and go after the people who hurt my daughter. But as I mentioned, it would have only embarrassed and hurt her more. So I chose instead to show gentleness for her sake. To be gentle, we must not view ourselves as better than others. Rather than asserting superiority, someone who is gentle wants to help others, even when they have been done wrong. I could have claimed my authority over her as her mother and did what I wanted to do. But by choosing to adhere to her wishes, I showed great strength in not retaliating and letting God handle what is His to control.

A great example of gentleness can be seen in John chapter 8 when the Pharisees brought the woman to Jesus who had been caught in adultry. The Pharisees told Jesus that the law of Moses commanded them to stone such a woman, to which Jesus responded, "Let the one of you who is without sin be the first to throw a stone." (paraphrased). After everyone left, Jesus did not condemn the woman; He instead says to her, "Go now and sin no more,"

In the same way that Jesus was gentle with this woman, He is also gentle with us. Even in our sins, He continues to love us. Christ does not keep a record of our wrongs but offers forgiveness if we come to Him. For this reason, He wants us to be gentle with others. Matthew 6:14-15 says, *"For if you forgive others when they sin against you, your heavenly Father will also forgive you. But if you do not forgive others their sins, your Father will not forgive your sins.*

A gentle heart comes from loving others; this is shown in our thoughts and interactions with those around us. So, how do we grow in gentleness? First, it is essential to perceive what gentleness is accurately. It should not be seen as a weakness but rather a strength. We can work toward becoming gentle when we see it this way.

In addition, it is vital to acknowledge how Christ is gentle with us. He is the creator of the universe, yet He is still delicate and loving towards us despite our sinful nature. Finally, we can incorporate gentleness into our own lives through prayer. We can ask Christ to give us a spirit of gentleness and take away feelings of self-righteousness. We can ask Him to reveal ways to show gentleness to others so we may reflect His character.

Thoughts to Ponder

Show Goodness

Let your light so shine before men, that they may see your good works, and glorify your Father which is in heaven.
                                                    Matthew 5:16

_____

Choices

Standing at a crossroad,
Which way should I go?
One looks good to me,
But a still soft voice tells me no.
Do I listen to this voice;
Or choose the one I like?
Because this one looks easy,
And the other like a rough hike.
So, I take the one most trodden,
But, oh what a terrible mistake!
This road leads to nowhere,
Only filled with grief and heartbreak.
It looks like I'm doomed,
I can't find my way out!
Oh, how I wish,
I had taken the other route.
Then Jesus softly whispers
I'm here, take my hand.
I reached up, as he reached down,
He led me out of the sinking sand.
From now on
I will listen to His voice,
Not my way, but His way
Will forever be my choice.
By: Karen Gaines

Scriptures in both the New and Old Testament tell us of the goodness of God. It is who He is, and He created us to show His goodness to those around us. We can see God's goodness daily—in how He guides us, protects us, and favors us. The goodness of God is a promise that believers can rely on entirely.

But are we living up to the example He has put before us? As women of God, are we guiding others? Are we protecting others? Do we show favor toward others? Just like we, as believers, can rely on God's goodness, others should also be able to rely on our goodness. It is what we are called to do.

So often, we forget what Christ did for us. I chose the poem at the beginning of this chapter to remind us just what that was. Do you remember a time that this was you? Do you remember that feeling of loneliness and despair that you were in when Christ found you? Then God, in His goodness and mercy, pulled you out.

I still remember the person God sent to help guide me back to Him. She didn't judge me, ridicule me for the wrongs I was doing, or try to force me to change. She only showed love, and acceptance towards me, and prayed with and for me. Her goodness let me see that not all Christians were judgmental and assertive.

See, I had been raised in church my entire life and had been hurt by church people. Therefore, I dodged such people as much as possible once I walked away. But this wonderful woman of God wasn't like that at all.

She showed me the true essence of how a woman of God should look and act. Just show goodness and kindness—that's all we are required to do. We're not other peoples' judge; only God can do that. We are to love them. Lead them to Christ by the example of what a faithful Christian is supposed to be—Christ-like.

Goodness

When you look up goodness, the definition is "the quality of being morally good or virtuous. Moral excellence; virtue. Kindly feeling, kindness; generosity.

Growing up, we are often told to "be good." Maybe this looked like helping your mom with chores or getting along with others in the school. I think the true meaning of goodness is commonly overlooked; because goodness is an action. It is not true goodness when we strive to be good only for our own benefit. True goodness is unselfish. It does not seek a reward.

Jesus Christ is a perfect example of goodness. He died on the cross for the sins of humanity. He did this to give us the gift of eternal life. Throughout His mission here on earth, He selflessly served others and became the ultimate sacrifice for sin—our sin, not His.

As women of God, we are called to live in a way that reflects the character of Christ. We don't do goodness to gain recognition. Often, the small act of kindness we do throughout our day means the most to those around us. When was the last time you wrote a short note or said an uplifting word to someone having a bad day? How about that person who is putting you down or scandalizing your name? Have you complained about it to your friends and huffed in anger? Wouldn't praying for them be better?

It is in these small acts of kindness that we reflect Christ the most. While it may seem to go unnoticed—God sees. And ultimately, He will show goodness to you. But, for now, rest in knowing that He sees—He knows—and He will reward. After all, you get back what you put out. So, don't live a miserable, beatdown life—walk in goodness, and goodness will come back to you.

We can't give out what we are given; by doing so, we bow to the enemy's devices. We all know who we are fighting. Satan will stop at nothing to see you down, don't give him that glory. Tell him you know who you are, and send him on his way. I'll end this chapter with this—Matthew 5:44-48, *But I say into you, Love your enemies, bless them that curse you, do good to them that hate you, and pray for them which despitefully use you, and persecute you; That ye may be the children of your Father which is in heaven: for he maketh his sun to rise on the evil and on the good, and sendeth rain of the just and on the unjust. For if you love them which love you, what reward have ye? do not even the publicans the same? And if ye salute your brethren only, what do ye more than others? Do not the publicans so? Be ye therefore perfect, even as your Father which is in heaven is perfect.*

Things to Ponder

Are You Faithful?

The heart of her husband doth safely trust in her, so that he shall have no need of spoil.
 She will do him good and not evil all the days of her life
Proverbs 31:11-12

Faithful to You

My faithfulness is to
You oh Lord,
To dare try it without you,
I cannot afford.
You make the sun to rise each day
And go down again,
You keep count of the hair on my head
And even the grains of sand.
You are always with me
Helping me make it through,
I am forever grateful and
Will always stand true.
I will be faithful to you
As on this journey I go,
And show your love to others
So that you they come to know.
By: Karen Gaines

Psalm 110:5 tells us, *"For the Lord is good; his mercy is everlasting; and his truth endureth to all generations."* This verse reminds us that no matter what we go through, we can always count on God's love and faithfulness. In Lamentation 3: 22-23, we find there that it says, *"It is of the Lord's mercies that we are not consumed, because his compassions fail not. They are new every morning: great is thy faithfulness.* In other words, this verse reminds us that God's love and loyalty will sustain us even when we feel we can't go on.

God's faithfulness means He is always there for us, no matter what. He never abandons us and is always willing to forgive us. We can count on Him no matter what happens in our lives. Are we mirroring this to people in our lives? Are we constantly showing love, compassion, and understanding to those around us, or do circumstances cause you to ebb and flow with how you feel that day?

You never know what a person is going through. So, when you find yourself flip-flopping on how you react to a person based on how the day is going, you need to realign yourself to the word. Repent. And try again. It's easy to show the love of Christ when things are going well. However, it's needed most when we find out that person has been talking about us behind our backs. It's needed most when someone is hateful or rude to us. It's needed most when that person isn't acting as we think they should.

People around us need us always to show the attributes of Christ. What if God was that way with us? What if we couldn't rely on His faithfulness to always come through for us? Think about this as you go about your day. How faithful are you to Him? How faithful are you when it comes to portraying the love of Christ to others?

Faithfulness

The definition given for faithfulness is the quality of being faithful. Loyalty, constancy, devotion, dedication, commitment, steadfastness, and allegiance are a few words.

When we tie this into what we have learned already—it means being all that—all the time. It's easy to slip into a mindset of doubt and cynicism. Your life, to this point, may be broken, and you may have lost trust in others who caused you to go through some painful experiences. For this reason, faithfulness can be a challenging trait to possess.

As a woman of God, it's essential to be faithful to God. But believing in Him is not enough; you must be faithful to Him. When you become truly faithful to Him, it will shape the way you live your entire life. We then can be loyal to those we come in contact with and truly show the love of Christ.

Faithfulness requires that we submit entirely to Christ in all our ways. This comes from a place of realizing that we are in need of a Savior and that He is in control of every aspect of our lives. I'll leave you with Proverbs 19:21. *"There are many devices in a man's heart; nevertheless the counsel of the Lord, that shall stand."* We are faithful to Christ because He is faithful to us. That means staying faithful, even when faced with opposition from others.

Thought to Ponder

_____
_____
_____
_____
_____
_____
_____
_____
_____

Meekness is not Weak

But sanctify the Lord God in your hearts: and be ready always to give an answer to every man that asketh you a reason of the hope that is in you with meekness and fear:
1 Peter 3:15

_____

Make Me Invisible

Make me Invisible Lord,
When they look my way
don't let them see me,
Hide me behind the cross,
Let it be you that they see.
Make me Invisible Lord,
Guard my mouth against words
that hurt or bruise,
Shape and mold me
into someone you can use
Make me Invisible Lord
Help me stand brave and
strong at all cost,
Let your love shine through me
so it might save one that's lost.
Make me Invisible Lord
A vessel of honor
that's tried and true,
Today and everyday
Let my life honor you.

By: Karen Gaines

A spiritually meek person is not self-willed—not continually concerned with their ways, ideals, and wishes. Instead, a meek person is willing to put themselves in second place and submit themselves to achieve what is good for others. Therefore, you might say that meekness opposes self-will, self-interest, and self-assertiveness. In other words—meekness isn't about "I"; meekness doesn't look inward at self; it looks outward at others.

Meekness is not synonymous with temperance or self-control, although it does require self-control to restrain or hold back exercising power or will over another person. Instead, a meek person controls her will and desire to please and submit to God's will and desire. So then, by submitting to God—He brings His blessing, as He takes us in our meek, submissive, humble hearts towards Him and rewards us by exalting us—elevating us to His glory.

He doesn't want us to submit to Him and ignore our relationships with others. When we demonstrate meekness, gentleness, and longsuffering with others, we are displaying the heart of Christ. This maintains a spirit of peace within us—with Christ—and living peaceably with all men and women. You can't do this when you are self-focused.

Jesus Christ is our best example of how meekness should look. Consequently, He told us He was meek and demonstrated it through His willingness to bear our heavy burdens for us. He exhibited extraordinary meekness by enduring so much pain for us—with no thought of self and without any complaint. During His crucifixion, He had the power and ability to release thousands of angels at any moment, yet—He refrained to atone and redeem humanity.

What a sacrifice! What an example to follow! As we look at what Jesus did, we can see that meekness is not about giving up power but rather diligently harnessing it for the good of others. In other words—you must decide to act meek. It's not innate. I guess you could say that what it comes down to is—what source you choose to follow—God or the world?

All you have to do is turn on the television, pick up a magazine, or watch people at your local supermarket—most everyone today is about self. I will use an example that most of us can relate to—you are standing in a long line at the checkout. You've been standing there a while. Then suddenly, this person comes up and steps in front of you. If you're like me, you don't say anything. But they have this attitude that they are special, and you owe them that right to break in the line. I don't have to tell you who this person is thinking about at this moment. They don't care if you have been there thirty minutes awaiting your turn. They only know they don't want to go to the end of the line.

Don't be that person. I chose the poem at the beginning of this chapter to point out what I want Christ to do in my life. Hide me behind the cross—in other words—let my actions and words match what Christ would do. When we submit ourselves to Him, it is easy to submit to others. As I've already mentioned, being meek does not mean you are weak. Not at all! Because it takes a lot of strength to be meek. A power that only Christ can give. Meekness may be among the most ununderstood words in the Bible. Meekness is courageous, not timid; strong, not weak; restrained, not excessive; active, not passive; modest, not self-seeking; gracious, not brash. A meek person isn't jealous of others but instead acknowledges the accomplishments they've achieved. A meek person isn't overbearing or easily provoked.

A meek person will be bold but not harsh. You will be courageous because you fear God more than flesh. That is why I said that you first must submit to Christ. As you do so, you know how to respond to any situation. He is there to guide you through it. When you let God speak through you, the message will be delivered with His power and authority, not your own. I'm going to end with this bible verse. Matthew 5:44—*But I say unto you, Love your enemies, bless them that curse you, do good to them that hate you and pray for them which despitefully use you, and persecute you;*

That is meekness.

.

Thoughts to Ponder

Self-control

For the grace of God that bringeth salvation hath appeared to all men, Teaching us that , denying ungodliness and worldly lusts, we should live soberly, righteously, and godly, in this present world; Looking for that blessed hope, and the glorious appearing of the great God and our Saviour Jesus Christ; Who gave himself for us, that he might redeem us from all iniquity, and purify unto himself a peculiar people, zealous of good works.

Titus 2:11-14

Saving Me

You say I'm nothing but selfish
For leaving you in destruction,
But I was losing control
Of my own construction.
You made it all about you
Never thinking of me,
I even carved it in my skin
But yet you didn't see.
So, I had to walk away
To save me from you
I hope in time you realize
It was what I had
To do.
By: Kiara Espinoza

Temperance is the last of the fruit of the Spirit. Words like moderation, restraint, self-discipline, and self-control describe the practice of temperance. We all understand that self-control guides us in enjoying good things in balanced moderation. We can become overly attached or even addicted to essentially good and pleasurable items. We see this in overweight people who do not discipline themselves regarding food—alcoholics or drug addicts who abuse these substances. However, I want to look deeper at what temperance means to a Christian.

Temperance enables you to control your basic human desires and natural impulses towards food, lust, and any other pleasurable drive you may experience. As women of God, that means keeping all the other fruit of the Spirit active in our lives. We do this by staying in the word (the Bible) and having a solid prayer life. We must let God control our lives to choose the good in every moment. A woman who is distant from Christ is also distant from herself. Christ must be the center of all you are. Seeking Him for every choice or decision is the most unambiguous indication of our commitment to Him and the appropriate means for Him to act in us and for His grace to transform us.

Now let's look at temperance, or self-control, as it applies to the subject of this book. It's easy to be loving and joyful toward people when everything is going well. However, what about those days when things aren't going so well? What about when you are feeling down or inadequate? What about when people are coming against us or things aren't going our way? What about those days?

Bad days are going to happen. They are inevitable. When you're already late, you will have someone cut you off in traffic. You will run into a clerk at the grocery store who is having a bad day, and she gets a rude attitude with you. Your neighbor may say something to your children that you don't like. Your co-worker may be upset with something they do or don't do. This list is endless.

Do you respond in rudeness or anger back to these situations? Because the truth is we are all fighting some battle. That car that cut you off could be a mother who hasn't had sleep for a while because the baby isn't sleeping well. She may not have seen you. That store clerk could have been dealing with attitudes from customers all day, and she misunderstood what you were asking her. Whatever the reason, a woman of God always responds in love—or we should.

Anger is one of the most challenging emotions to keep in check. But we all must work on keeping it under submission a little better. However, it is only one strong emotion that we need to keep in line. Others include lust, hunger, envy, malice, hatred, resentment, fear, pride, and desire. If we don't learn to practice temperance in these areas, we will constantly clash with others around us.

When we lust after things other people have that we don't, it opens the door for envy. Resentment starts to rise within us. Malice takes over our thoughts. Then we start saying or doing things to people that shouldn't be found in a woman of God's mind. That's when we begin nit-picking and finding faults in others and pointing them out—petty things, as I mentioned in earlier chapters. We see something in them that makes us feel inadequate, so we choose to tear them down for no reason—this has to stop!

By applying temperance, we must train ourselves to stop and think about why we feel the need to harm others. James 3: 5-10 states, *Even so the tongue is a little member, and boasteth great things. Behold, how great a matter a little fire kindleth! And the tongue is a fire, a world of iniquity: so is the tongue among our members, that it defileth the whole body, and setteth on fire the course of nature; and it is set on fire of hell. For every beast, and of the birds, and of the serpents, and of the things in the sea, is tamed, and hath been tamed of mankind: But the tongue can no man tame; it is an unruly evil, full of deadly poison. Therewith bless we God, even the Father; and therewith curse we men, which are made after the similitude of God. Out of the same mouth proceedeth blessings and cursing. My brethren these things ought not so to be.*

We can use our words to move towards doing something wrong or something right. With our words, we can influence people to begin something tremendous or towards forming something evil. Our words can point someone in the right direction or get them started in the wrong direction. There is power in your words. You can bring life or death into your life, or someone else's, by what you say and how you say it. Everything you think or feel--does not need to be said.

In verse above, James tells us that it takes only a small statement to start a larger wickedness. He's trying to say to us just how hurtful and destructive our words can be if not guarded and controlled. Ecclesiastes chapter 5, verse 6 tells us not to let our mouth make us sin. Then in Psalm 141:3-4, we find, *Set a watch, O Lord, before my mouth; keep the door of my lips. Incline not my heart to any evil thing, to practice wicked works with men that work iniquity: and let me not eat of their dainties.*

Here in Psalm, we have been given a great prayer by David. He doesn't start by asking God to deliver him from his enemies or strike them down in judgment. Instead, he prays first for his mouth and heart. David may have been inclined to retaliate against Saul. After all, David was on the run for his life for ten years. But, facing danger, he pleaded with God for self-control. Our hearts, like David's, are naturally inclined to evil. However, here in Psalm 141, we find a man who knows this about his own heart, at least enough to know it is dangerous if left unbound. He knows he needs the constraints God sets and the Holy Spirit's restraining power.

We need to do the same. We need to stay focused on Christ in prayer. Concentrate on what needs mending in our own lives; then, we wouldn't be pointing out the fault and flaws of others. Instead, we would realize that we all are broken and need a Savior. Wouldn't it be great to look for the good in others instead of always pointing out the bad? What if we prayed for our enemies and looked for opportunities to love them instead of retaliating? What if we held our tongue more often instead of lashing out in the heat of the moment? What if we realized that we are all perfectly imperfect and love those differences in each other?

Lord, help my shortcomings—our shortcomings. Set a guard, O Lord, over my mouth; keep watch over the door of my lips! Do not let my heart incline to any evil, to busy myself with wicked deeds in company with people who practice immoral or grossly unfair behavior, and let me not be lured into their pleasure of sin!

Thoughts to Ponder

_____
_____
_____
_____
_____
_____
_____
_____

Final Thoughts

For the grace of God that bringeth salvation hath appeared to all men, Teaching us that , denying ungodliness and worldly lusts, we should live soberly, righteously, and godly, in this present world; Looking for that blessed hope, and the glorious appearing of the great God and our Saviour Jesus Christ; Who gave himself for us, that he might redeem us from all iniquity, and purify unto himself a peculiar people, zealous of good works.
Titus 2:11-14

Restored

Soft skin,
Pale eyes,
Oh, what a sinful demise.
so pure, for you cannot hide
from this cruel world filled
with harsh jokes and lies.
Those once soft eyes
Are now hard and cold,
for this cruel, harsh world
has stolen your soul.
But they can't keep
you down for long,
soon you will
sing a happy song.
What they stole
Jesus will restore,
He'll turn their destruction
into your greatest reward.
By: Kiara Espinoza

We've all been broken, beaten down, and bruised. Like me, I'm sure you have a few scars from life's battles. First, I want to say—stop picking at the wounds and let God heal them. Stop letting your past—or people in your present- tell you who you are or are not! Stop using your past experiences to push people away or hurt them by saying nasty things about them. Stop talking about or hurting other people just because they acquire a feature, talent, or object that you don't.

I'm not trying to sound preachy or authoritative over you and your life in a judgmental fashion. I'm speaking from experience. I can't say I've never spoken ill of a person—because I have. I also can't say that harsh words haven't hurt me from others—they have. I have been on both sides of the fence. However, I'm not too fond of drama. So, I can say that I have spent more time on the side that caused hurt to me, more than I have hurt others.

I've spent many years listening to the awful lies and comments made about me that I forgot who I was. Unfortunately, I had started believing these things, which resulted in living a life so full of hate and self-destruction that I had just about given up. I don't want that to be you. Don't waste another minute letting other people define who you are.

You can start this by asking Christ to come into your heart. Ask Him to forgive you of all your sins. Ask

Him to show you who you are in Him. An excellent place to start is in the Word. First, buy yourself a Bible if you don't have one. I suggest a KJV; that is the most accurate version. Next, surround yourself with Christ-minded people; get away from those that only want to sow discord and hurt.

Learn to love like Christ. Love covers a multitude of sins (1 Peter 4:8 And above all things have fervent charity (love) among yourselves: for charity (love) shall cover a multitude of sins.). In this verse, Peter describes how Christians should respond when faced with persecution. Take on Christ's attitude and expect God's purpose for your life to include suffering. Yet, in this suffering, you still show love to others. You still display forth the attributes of who Christ is—not the opposite.

Fervent charity (love) means to love wholeheartedly; this is demonstrated by forgetting the mistakes and stumbling of others rather than harboring grudges or reminding ourselves and others of past imperfections. Matthew 22: 37-38 explains this concept. *Jesus said unto him, Thou shalt love the Lord thy God with all thy heart, and with all thy soul, and with all thy mind. This is the first and great commandment. And the second is like unto it, Thou shalt love thy neighbor as thyself. On these two commandments hang all the law and the prophets.* It is difficult to sin against God or people if love is active in our life.

When we learn to love like Christ, we not only love ourselves and others alike. We understand that His love is not dependent on feelings; it is given whether it is accepted or not. We love selflessly because we know Christ will multiply His love toward us when we love others freely. In other words, we are rewarded for loving like Him. His love for us is the greatest of all rewards ever given.

However, you need to keep in mind that loving others is often misunderstood as an emotion. Although emotions can be part of it, the love you need to express is an action. It is an attitude about life, God, and the people around us that drives us to do good. That's the covering of a multitude of sins—think about it—what sins can be committed when we stay conscious of loving God and each other with deep love? Can you hate while you love? No. Can you harm or hurt your fellow sisters in Christ while you love? No. Can you lie, cheat, or steal when you believe in Christ, strive to be like Him, and love like Him? No

And lastly, you may be like me; you may have received more hurt than you dished out-- Love them anyway. Christ loved you when you were at your worst. Forgive them—He forgave you. Love them—He loved you. And He loves them. They just haven't come to realize that yet. So everywhere you go, every person you encounter—show them what the love of Christ looks like. Let His love shine through you every day, everywhere you go—let it shine through in the things you do and say.

We should always strive to edify or lift each other, not tear each other down. So let's pray for those who hate us. Pray for your enemies; bless those that curse you. Pray for those that despitefully use you. Be merciful, judge not, condemn not—forgive. Give, and it shall be given back to you; good measure, pressed down and shaken together, and running over. (Matthew 5:44-47). And remember to be the imperfectly perfect woman of God that you have been called to be; be quick to straighten the crown of a fallen sister and help her back up, don't push her father down.

You are perfectly imperfect—you are God called—God appointed—God anointed—uniquely you. So walk in that call with your nose low but your head held high. Knowing that He who started a good work in you will perform it until the day of Jesus Christ. Be blessed—be a blessing.

Thoughts to Ponder

_____
_____
_____
_____
_____
_____
_____

Question to Help You Grow

What are some ways you can show love more?

To find true joy we must learn to trust in God and His promises. What are some areas, or things, that you need to place in His hands so that your joy may be full?

What are some things that you can do to bring more peace into your life and the lives of others?

What are some ways that you can begin to be more longsuffering with others?

What are some ways you can show gentleness with others?

What are some ways you can show goodness to others?

Name times that faithfulness needs to be practiced more often.

What are some ways you can show meekness more often?

_____

_____

_____

_____

_____

_____

What are some ways you can show temperance more?

_____

_____

_____

_____

_____

_____

Notes

OTHER BOOKS BY
AUTHOR KAREN PLESS GAINES
Find these books on Amazon.com

- The Long Road Home
- Lost in the Fall
- Raylene's Daughter

Notes
(Resources used)

❖ King James Bible
❖ Webster online Dictionary

www.ingramcontent.com/pod-product-compliance
Lightning Source LLC
Chambersburg PA
CBHW060204050426
42446CB00013B/2984